Peace Be With You

Words of Comfort

Written By Peggy Sneller

Great Quotations, Inc.

Cover Illustration by Design Dynamics
Typography by MarketForce, Burr Ridge, IL

Published by Great Quotations Publishing Co., Glendale Heights, IL

Library of Congress Catalog Number: 98-75439

ISBN: 1-56245-358-0

Printed in Hong Kong 2000

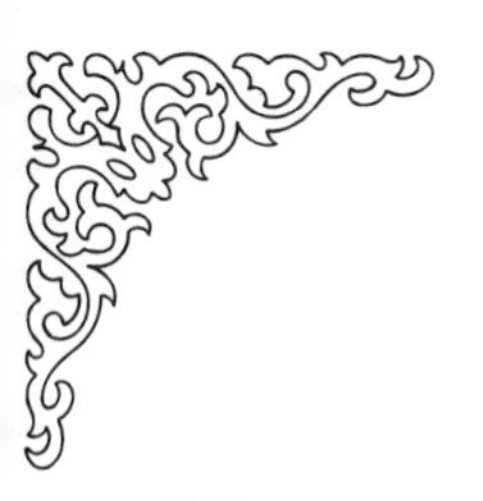

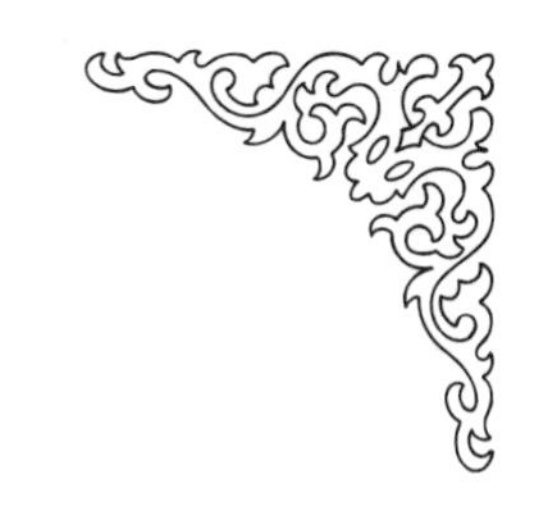

This book is dedicated with love and thanks to my family, especially to Marv, Brent, and Beth.

I pray that all who read these words of encouragement will find peace that only God can give.

...My God, my God,
why have you forsaken me?

Matthew 27:46

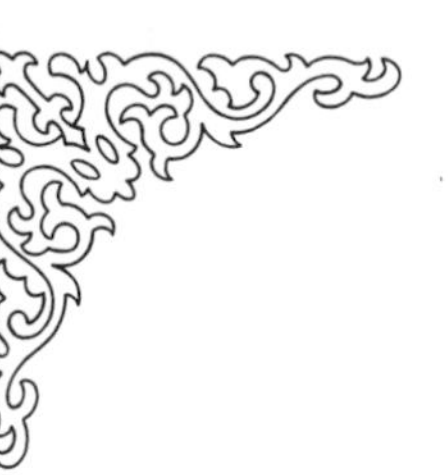

One night I had a dream. I was walking along the beach with the Lord, and across the skies flashed scenes from my life. In each scene I noticed two sets of footprints in the sand. One was mine, and one was the Lord's. When the last scene of my life appeared before me, I looked back at the footprints in the sand, and, to my surprise, I noticed that many times along the path of

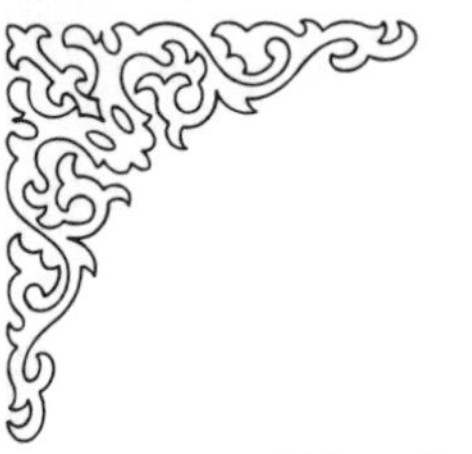

my life there was only one set of footprints. And I noticed that it was at the lowest and saddest times of my life. I asked the Lord about it: 'Lord, You said that once I decided to follow You, You would walk with me all the way. But I noticed that during the most troublesome times in my life there is only one set of footprints.

I don't understand why You left my side when I needed You most.' The Lord said: 'My precious child, I never left you during your time of trial. Where you see only one set of footprints, I was carrying you.'

Rejoice in the Lord always. I will say again: Rejoice!

Philippians 4:4

Jesus, You never promised to take away my burdens, but You did promise to help carry them. And I do rejoice in You because of what You did for me and what You still do for me anew each day.

...God Himself will be with them and be their God. He will wipe away every tear from their eyes.

Revelation 21:3,4

Too often I've kept my tears inside or allowed them to pour out only behind closed doors. Help me to remember I'm never alone. Others hold me up in prayer, and Your loving arms surround me.

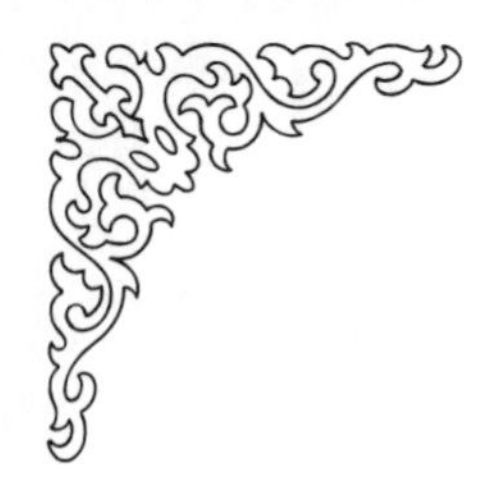

There is a time for everything
and a season for every activity
under heaven.

Ecclesiastes 3:1

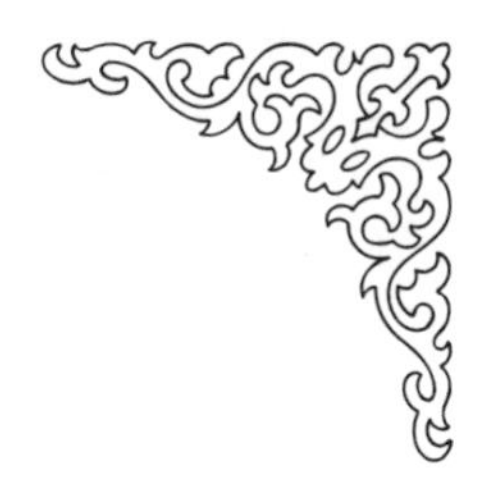

Your time is the right time, Lord. Blessings, too numerous to count, have been heaped upon me. Joy has filled my life. Now, in my time of sorrow, I put my hope in You for comfort, perseverance, and peace.

A time to be born, and a time to die...

Ecclesiastes 3:2

You give to us, Lord,
and You take away.
Blessed be Your name.

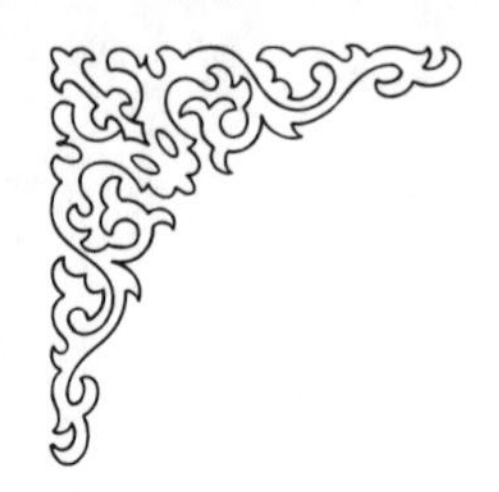

...A time to mourn and a time to dance.

Ecclesiastes 3:4

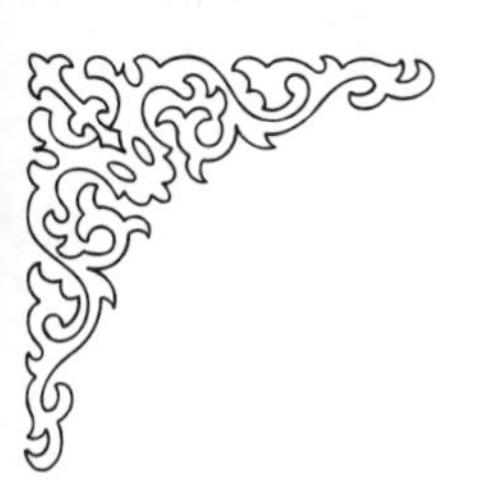

When Christ shall come with shouts of acclamation

And take me home, what joy shall fill my heart!

Then I shall bow in humble adoration

And there proclaim:
My God, how great Thou art.

Stuart Hine

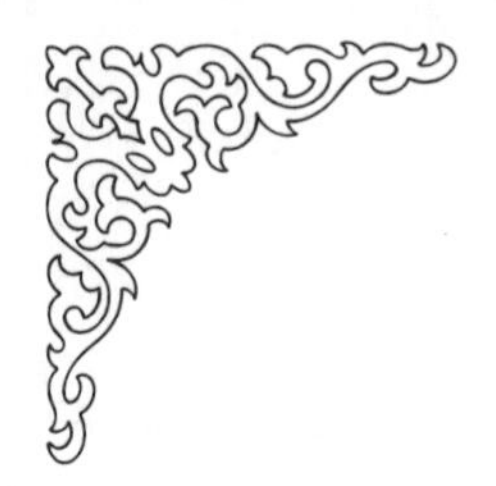

Now may the Lord of peace Himself give you peace at all times and in every way...

2 Thessalonians 3:16

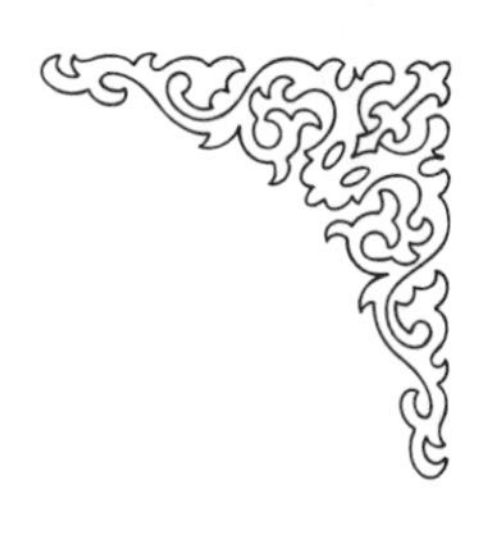

I've sunk to moments of deepest despair. Lord, grant me the peace and tranquility that I can't find for myself. They have to come from You. I cling to Your promises and place my hope in You.

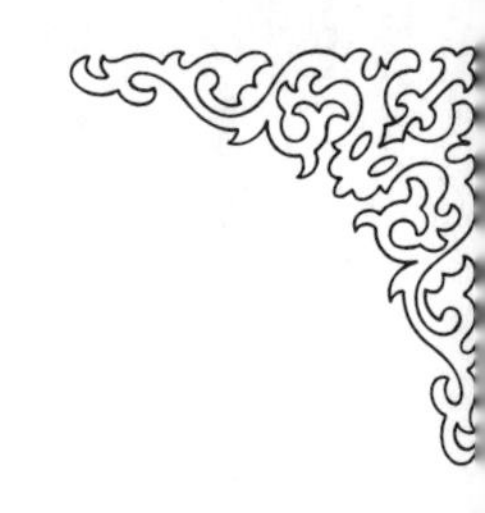

The Lord is gracious and righteous; our God is full of compassion.

Psalms 116:5

I bring all my needs to You because You do care for me. You cared enough to suffer and die. Since You gave Your life for me, I know You also care about my suffering. I look to You for peace.

You hear, O Lord, the desire of the afflicted, You encourage them, and You listen to their cry.

Psalms 10:17

Help me to be persistent in bringing my needs to You. Often, I have not because I ask not. Let Your peace fill my life.

Cast all your anxiety on Him because He cares for you.

1 Peter 5:7

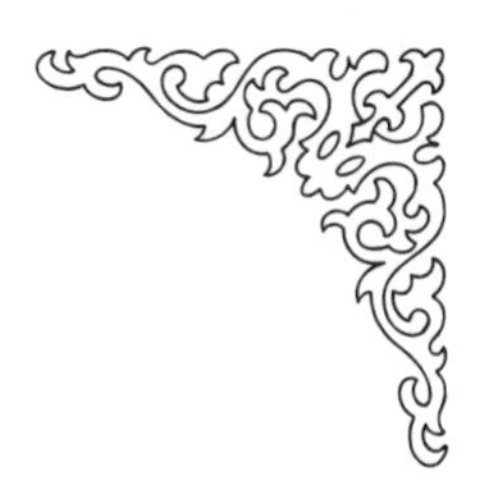

So cast your burden on
Him, Seek His counsel
when distressed,

And go to Him for comfort
When you're lonely
and oppressed.

Helen Steiner Rice

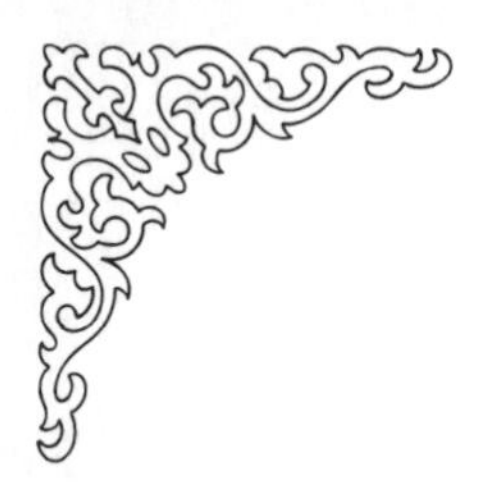

Pray continually.

1 Thessalonians 5:17

A prayer in its simplest definition is merely a wish turned God-ward.

Phillips Brooks

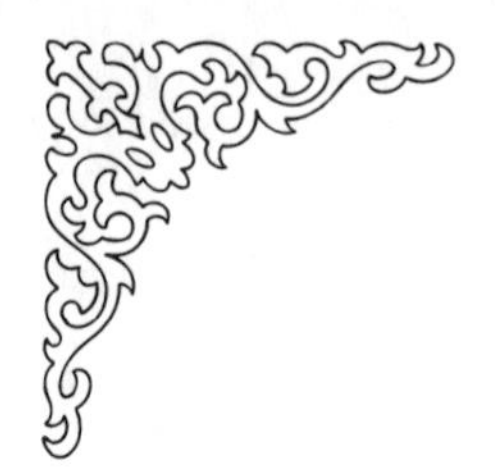

As a mother comforts her child, so will I comfort you.

Isaiah 66:13

Lord, help me to understand how You help me through each day - through a book, a story, a friend, someone to love, work to do, people who need me.

I will turn their mourning into gladness; I will give them comfort and joy instead of sorrow.

Jeremiah 31:13

Thru this world of toil
and snares,

If I falter, Lord, who cares?

Who with me my burden
shares?

None but Thee, dear Lord,
none but Thee.

Anonymous

But those who hope in the Lord will renew their strength. They will soar on wings like eagles; they will run and not grow weary, and they will walk and not be faint.

Isaiah 40:31

Even though I can't see the plan You have for me, Lord. I know You are closely watching over me as the Master Planner. In Your timing, everything fits together perfectly. What a comfort it is to know that You have a plan for my life.

Be still, and know that I am God...

Psalms 46:10

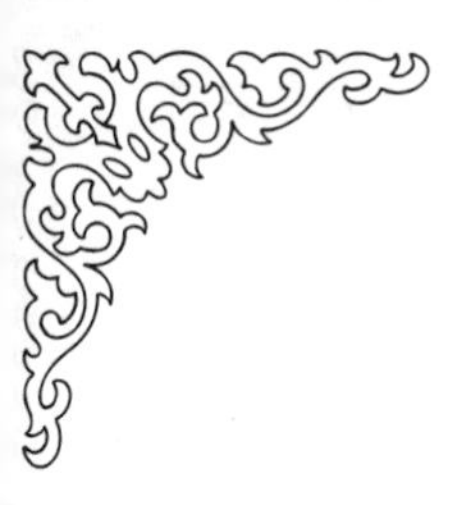

God is the friend of silence. Trees, flowers, grass grow in silence. See the stars, moon and sun, how they move in silence.

Mother Teresa

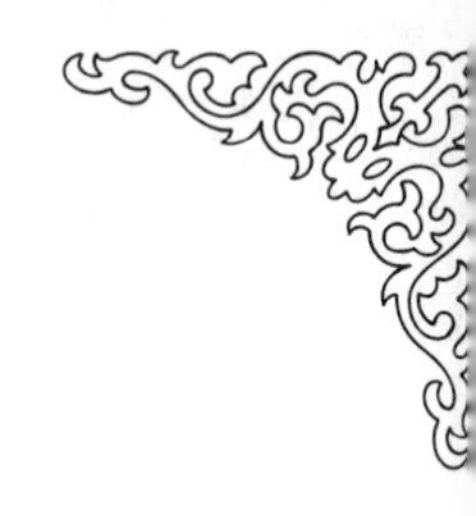

Trust in Him at all times,
O people; pour out your heart
to Him, for God is our refuge.

Psalms 62:8

It's precisely in letting go, in entering into complete union with the Lord, in letting Him take over, that we discover our true selves. It's in the act of abandonment that we experience redemption, that we find life, peace, and joy in the midst of physical, emotional, and spiritual suffering.

Joseph Cardinal Bernardin

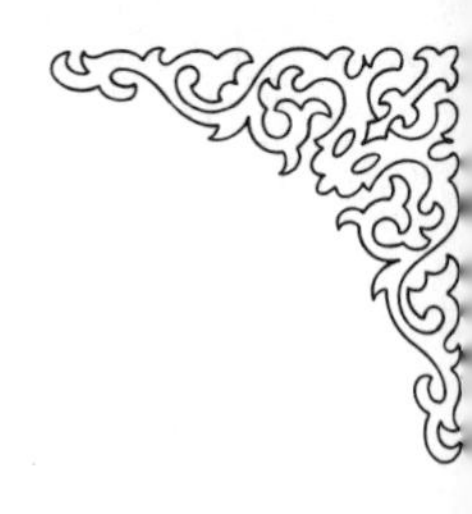

You will keep him in perfect peace, him whose mind is steadfast, because he trusts in You.

Isaiah 26:3

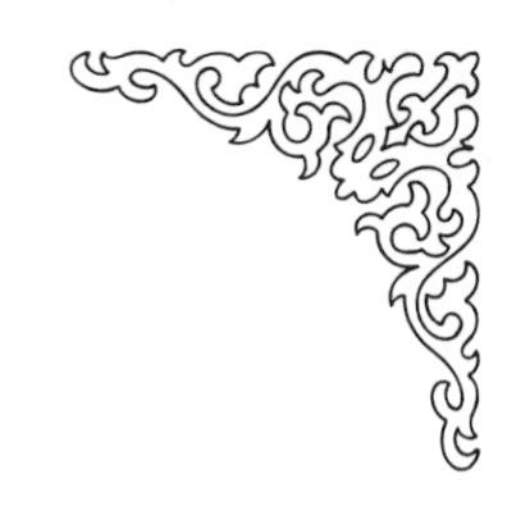

I am trusting You, Lord Jesus;
Never let me fall. I am trusting,
You forever and for all.

Frances R. Havergal

Out of the depths I cry to You, O Lord; O Lord, hear my voice. Let Your ears be attentive to my cry for mercy.

Psalms 130:1,2

You do understand, Lord that I am in the depth of despair. I feel deserted and forsaken by others. I bring my burden and sorrow to You.

You've promised to be there, when I seek You. Hear my prayer and draw me close to You.

Why are you downcast, O my soul? Why so disturbed within me: Put your hope in God...

Psalms 42:5

There is but one way to tranquility of mind and happiness, and that is to account no external things thine own, but to commit all to God.

Epictetus

Look at the birds of the air; they do not sow or reap or store away in barns and yet your heavenly Father feeds them. Are you not much more valuable than they?

Matthew 6:26

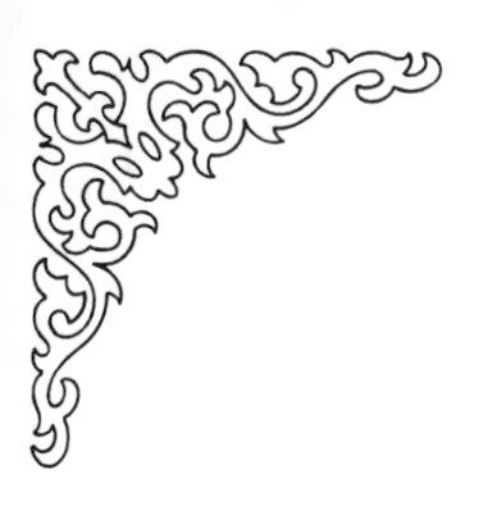

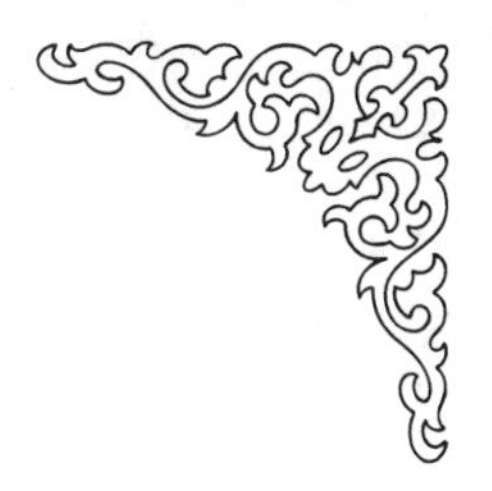

Dear Lord, help me to always know that as much as I loved the one I lost, even more so do You love me.

Therefore do not worry about tomorrow, for tomorrow will worry about itself. Each day has enough trouble of its own.

Matthew 6:34

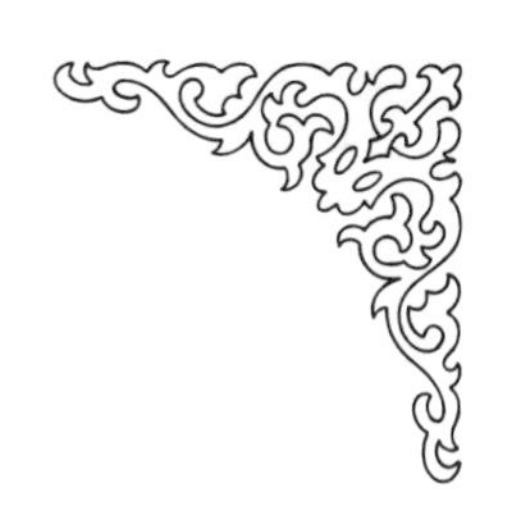

Do not look forward to what might happen tomorrow; the same everlasting Father who cares for you today will take care of you tomorrow and every day. Either He will shield you from suffering or He will give you unfailing strength to bear it. Be at peace then, and put aside all anxious thoughts and imaginations.

St. Francis de Sales

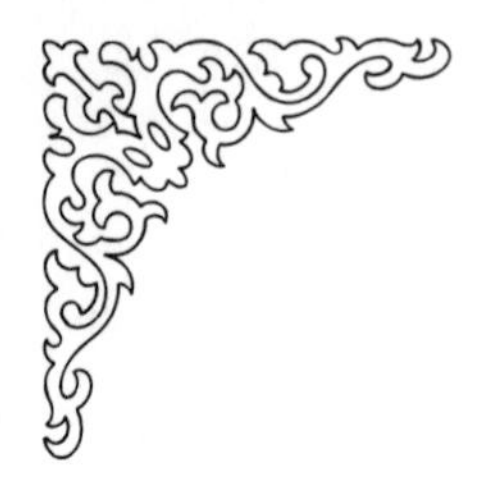

Come to Me, all of you who are weary and burdened, and I will give you rest.

Matthew 11:28

My heart is so heavy, and I'm so weary from the grief within me. I come to You to wipe away my tears and to hold me within Your loving arms.

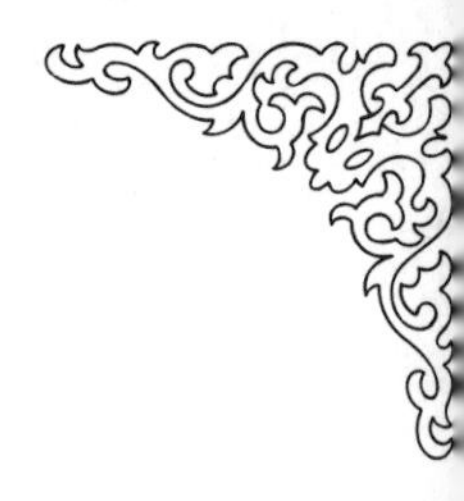

Even though I walk through the valley of the shadow of death, I will fear no evil, for You are with me: Your rod and Your staff, they comfort me.

Psalms 23:4

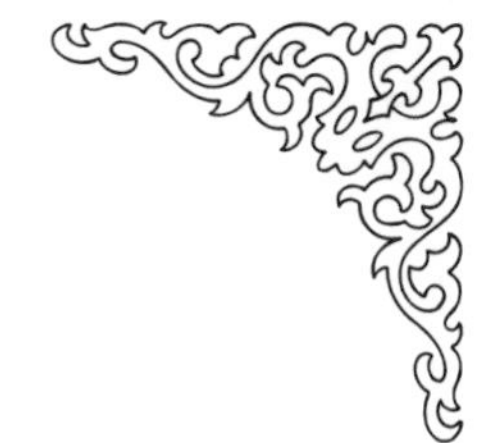

Neither life nor death can ever, from the Lord His children sever:

For His love and deep compassion comforts them in tribulation.

What He takes or what He gives us, shows the Father's love so precious;

We may trust His purpose wholly-'Tis His children's welfare solely.

Lina Sandell Berg

...The Lord will be your everlasting light, and your days of sorrow will end.

Isaiah 61:2

You, Lord, are the light at the end of this seemingly never ending, dark tunnel. I cling to Your promises that my sorrows will end.

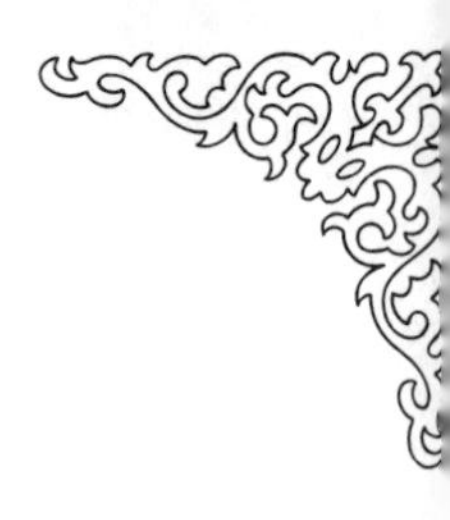

And the peace of God, which transcends all understanding, will guard your hearts and minds in Christ Jesus.

Philippians 4:7

When we are at peace, we find the freedom to be most fully who we are, even in the worst of times. We let go of what is nonessential and embrace what is essential. We empty ourselves so that God may more fully work within us. And we become instruments in the hands of the Lord.

Joseph Cardinal Bernardin

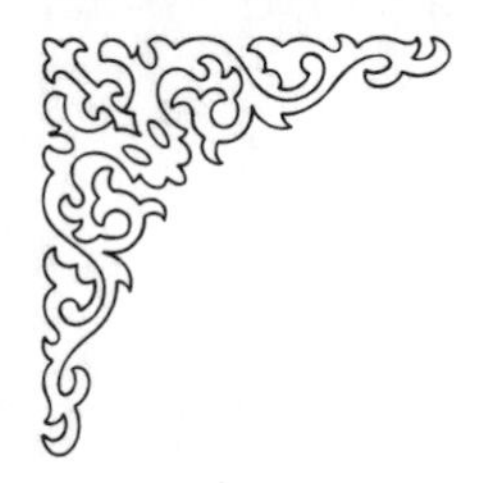

This is the day the Lord has made; let us rejoice and be glad in it.

Psalms 118:24

As the sun peeks over the horizon, a new day begins... a gift, a new opportunity for God to lighten my heavy heart, to bring rays of hope into my life, to warm my spirit.

Do not let your hearts be troubled. Trust in God; trust also in Me. In My Father's house are many rooms; if it were not so, I would have told you. I am going to prepare a place for you.

John 14:1, 2

If we could see beyond today
as God can see,
If all the clouds should roll
away, the shadows flee;
O'er present griefs we would
not fret,
Each sorrow we would soon
forget,
For many joys are waiting yet,
For you and me.

Anonymous

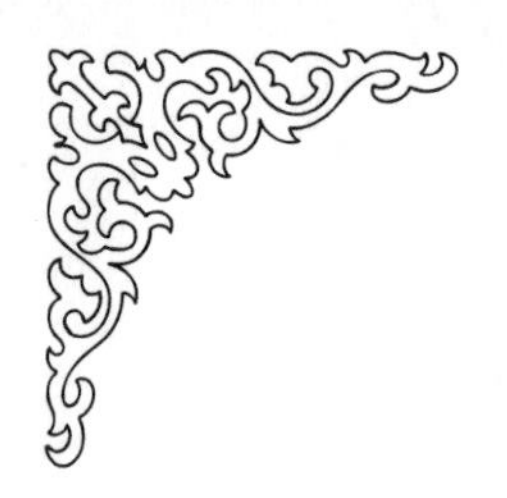

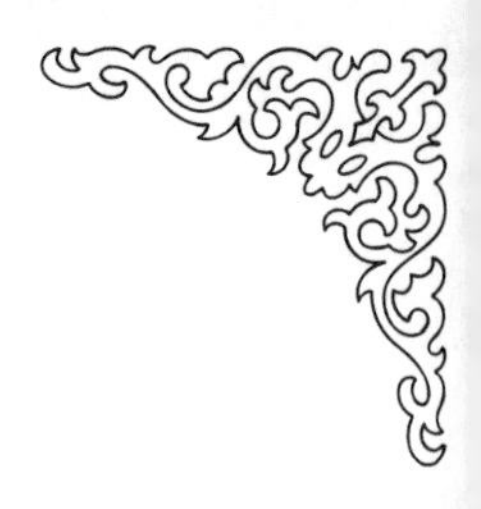

Neither will I leave you; never will I forsake you.

Hebrews 13:5

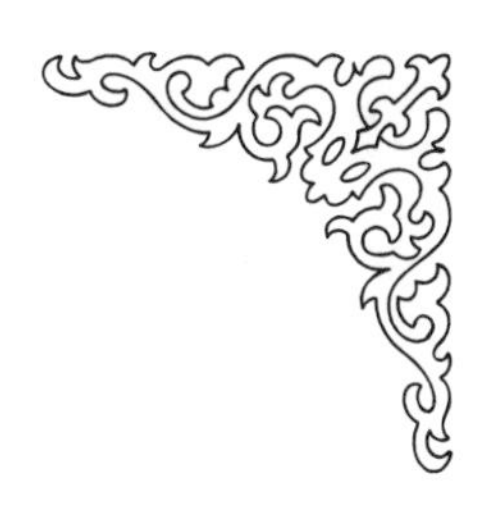

We must believe that the Lord loves us, embraces us, never abandons us (especially in our most difficult moments). This is what gives us hope in the midst of life's suffering and chaos.

Joseph Cardinal Bernardin

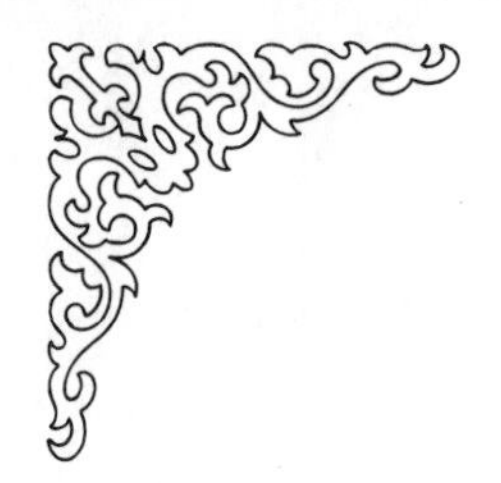

Peace I leave with you; My peace I give to you. I do not give to you as the world gives. Do not let your hearts be troubled and do not be afraid.

John 14:27

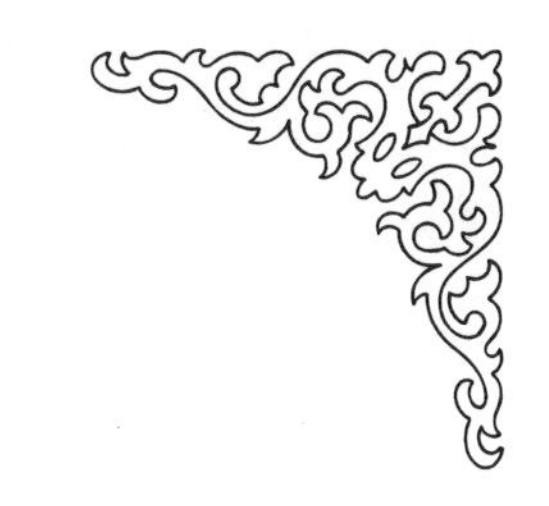

Lord, make me an
instrument of Your peace.
Where there is hatred, let me
sow love.
Where there is injury, pardon.
Where there is doubt, faith.
Where there is despair, hope.
Where there is darkness, light.
Where there is sadness, joy.

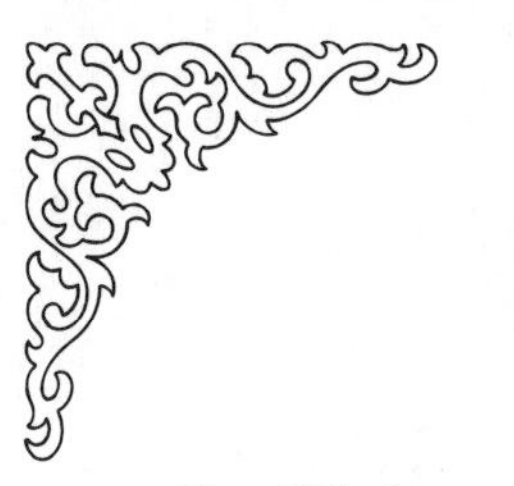

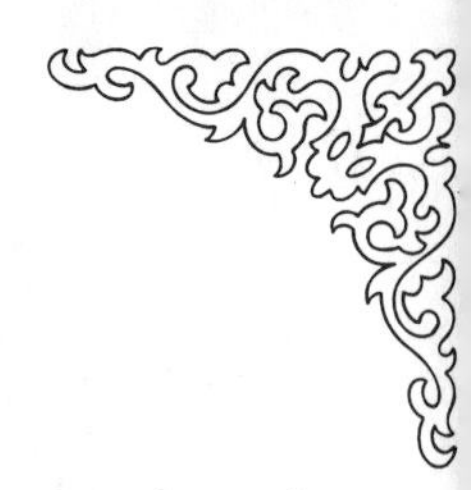

O, Divine Master, grant that I may not so much seek to be consoled, as to console;
to be understood, as to understand;
to be loved, as to love;
for it is in giving that we receive, it is in pardoning that we are pardoned. It is in dying that we are born to eternal life.

St. Francis of Assisi